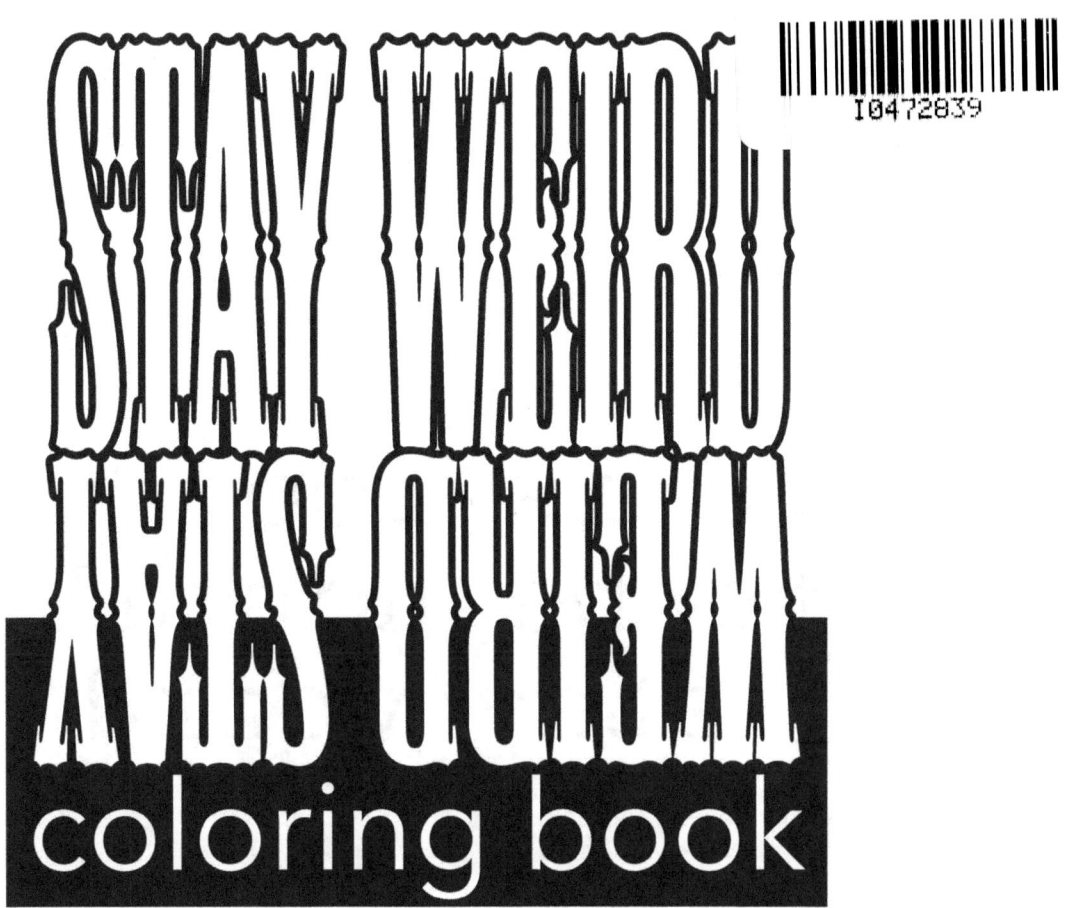

kate blume

ISBN: 978-0-6480847-3-0 BIC Subject category: 1. Drawing-coloring books for grown-ups 2. Arts & Photography- techniques
3. Craft, hobbies- art 4. Self-help-art therapy & relaxation 5. Self-help-anger management. 6.Self-help-stress relief

life is too short
to be normal,
stay weird

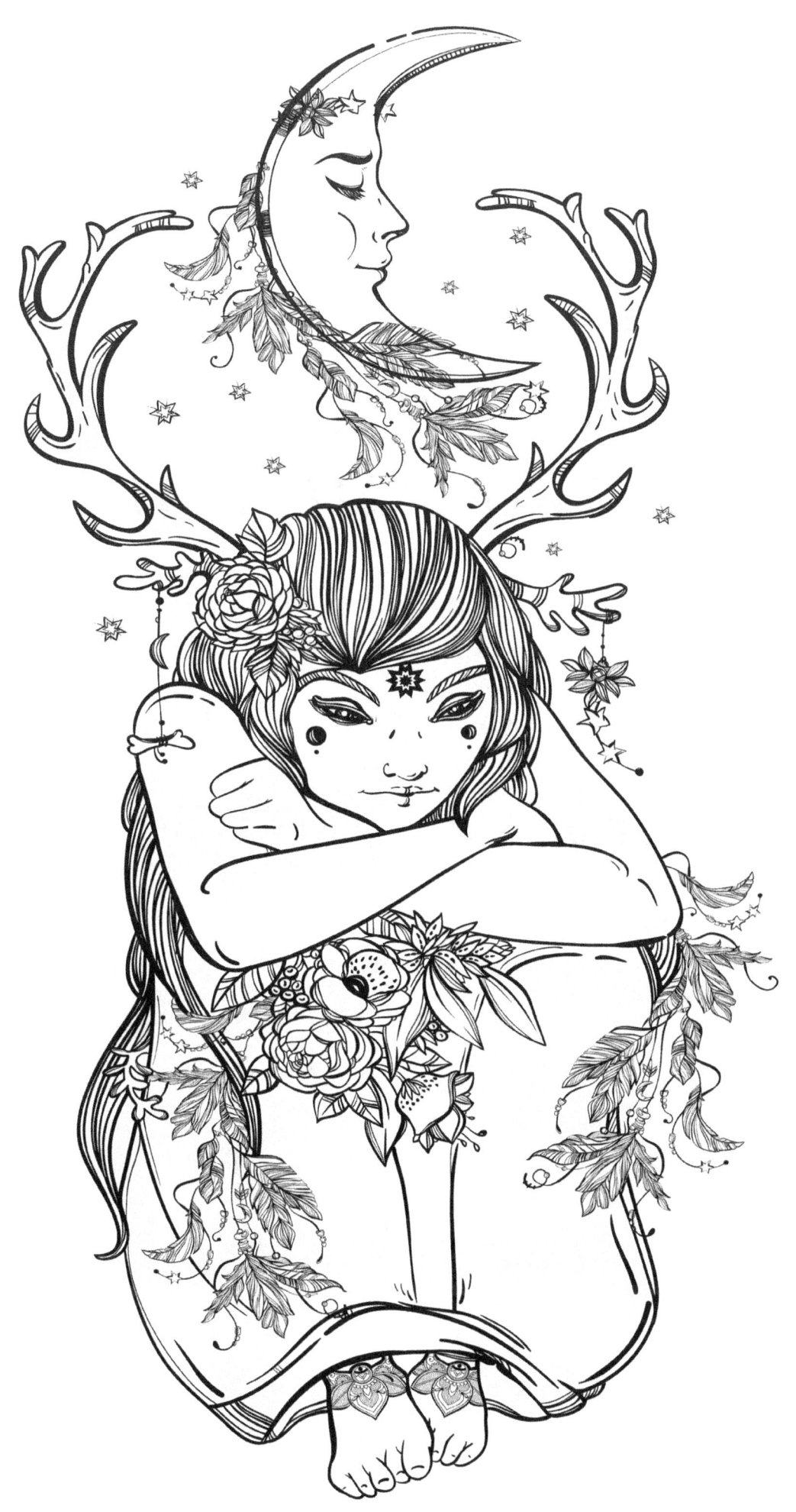

normal is
so fu*king boring

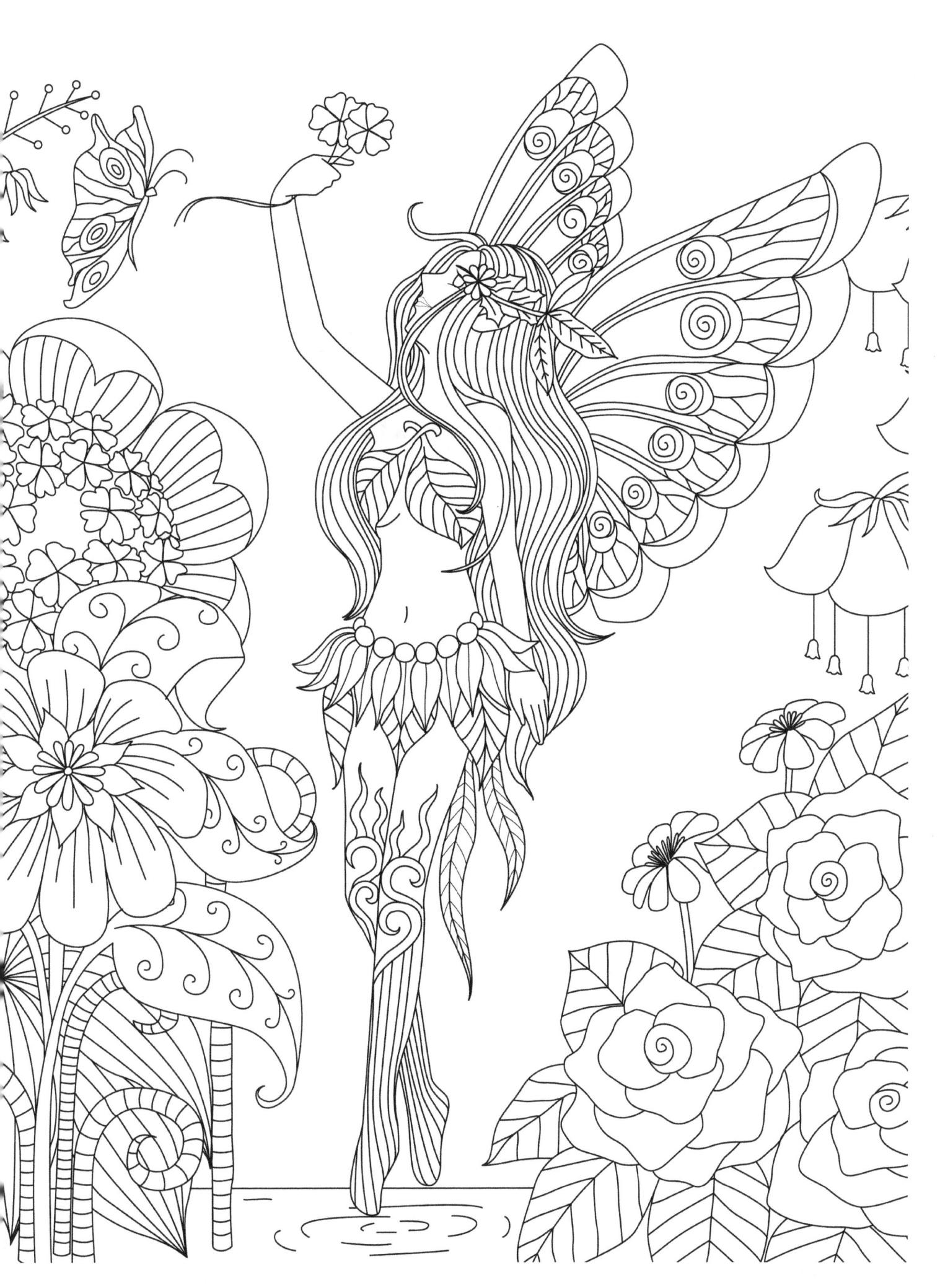

weird is
the new normal,
stay weird

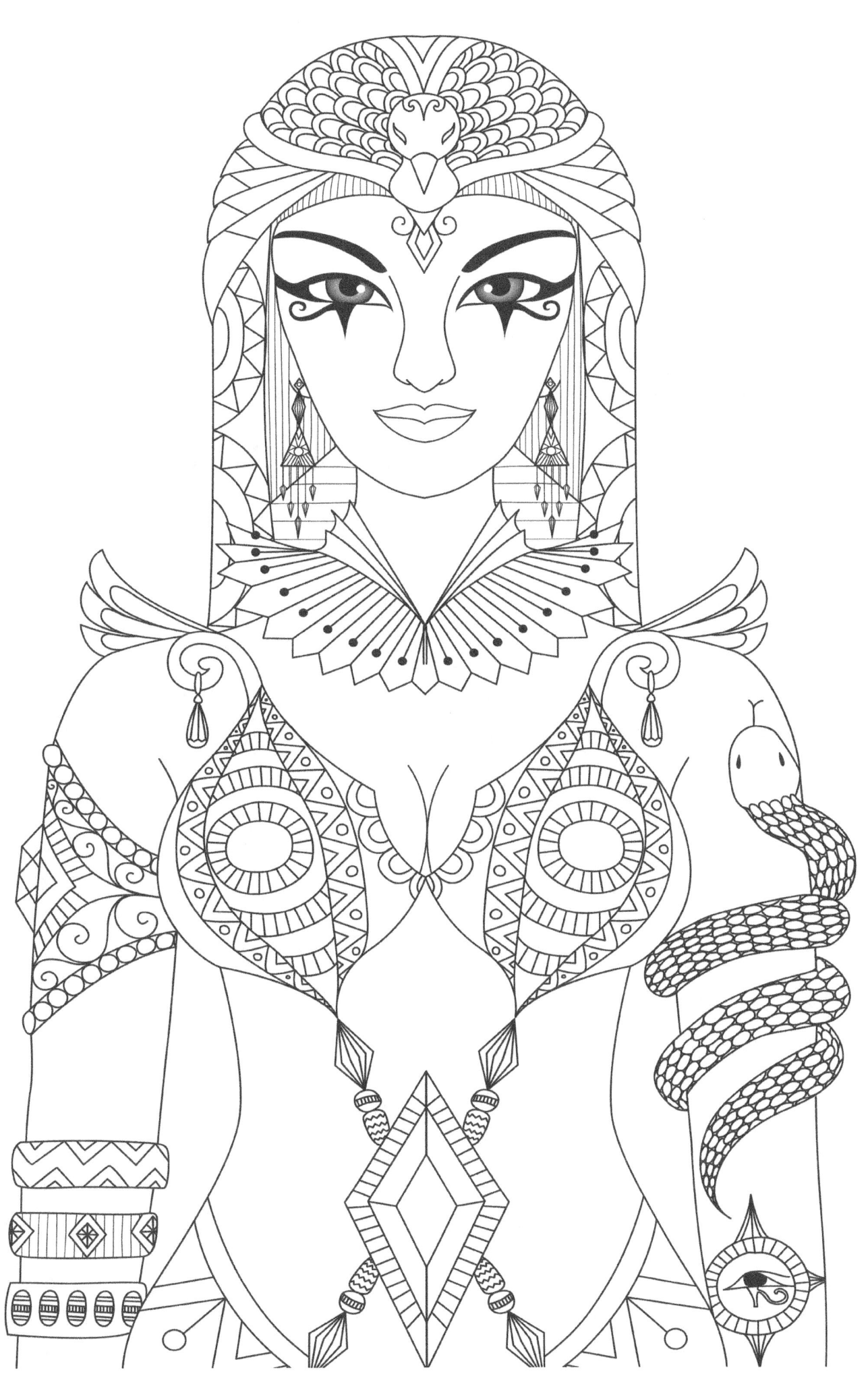

you're so weird
(don't change)

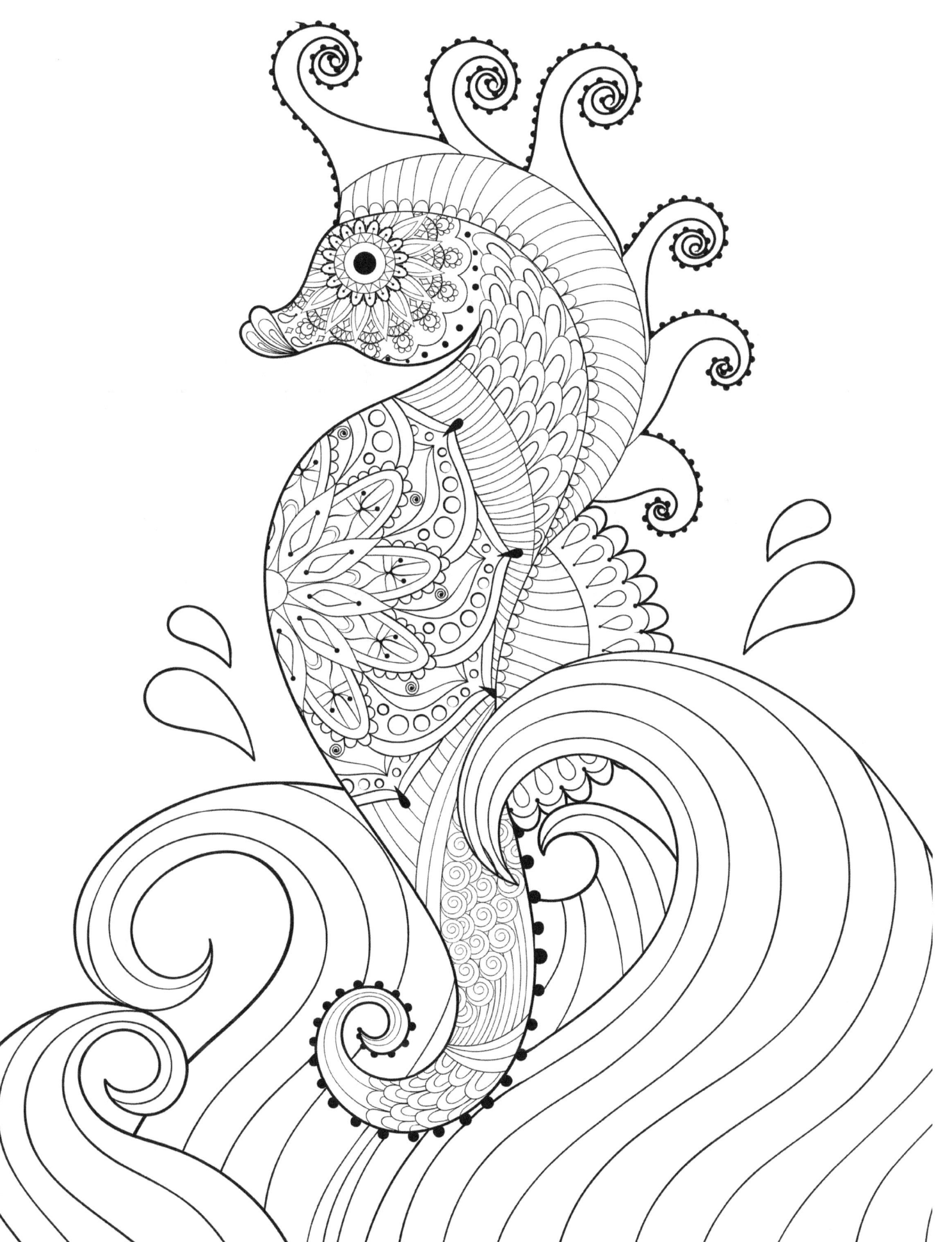

you laugh at me
because i'm different
I laugh at you
because you're all
the same

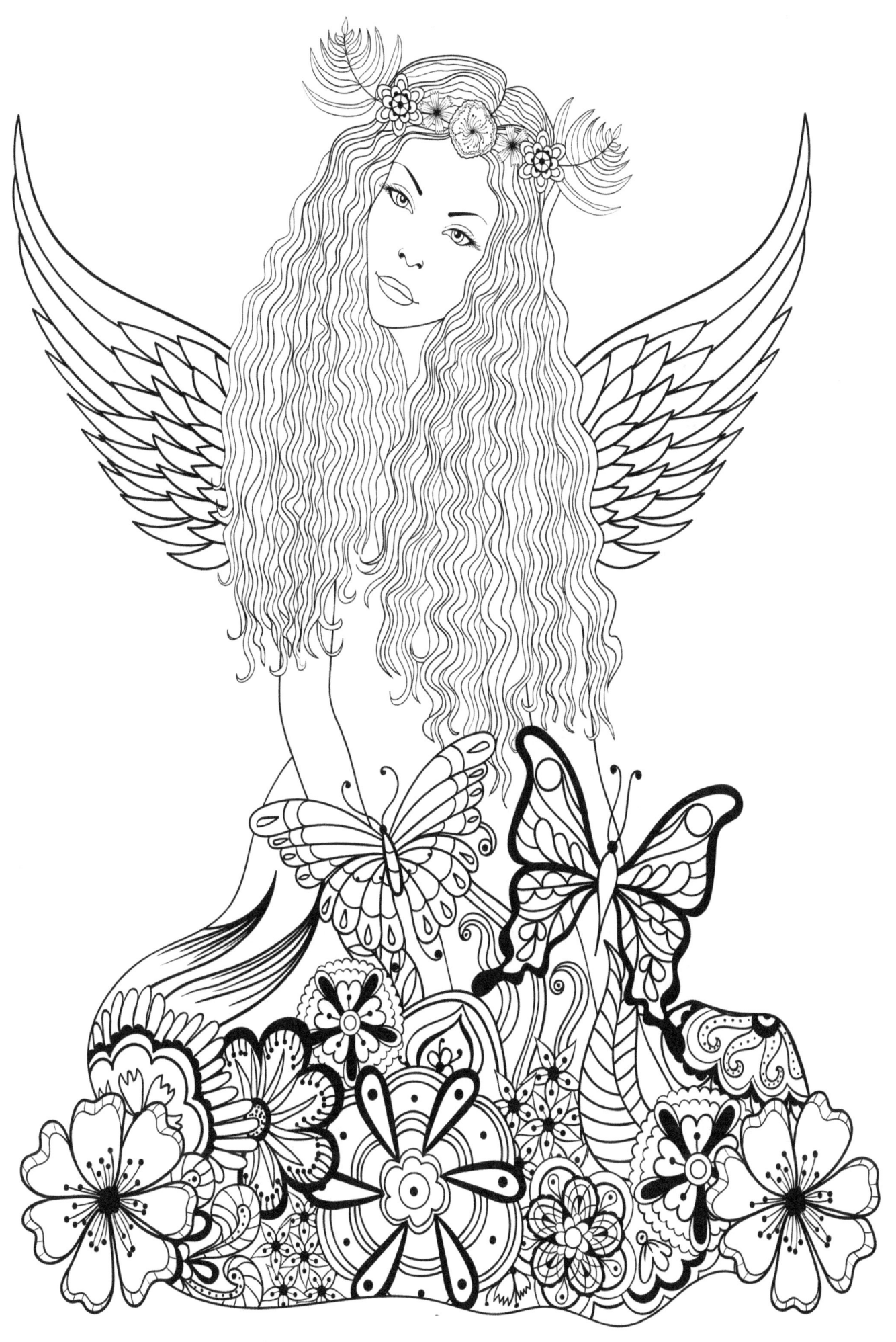

trust me, as you get
to know me, i just
get weirder

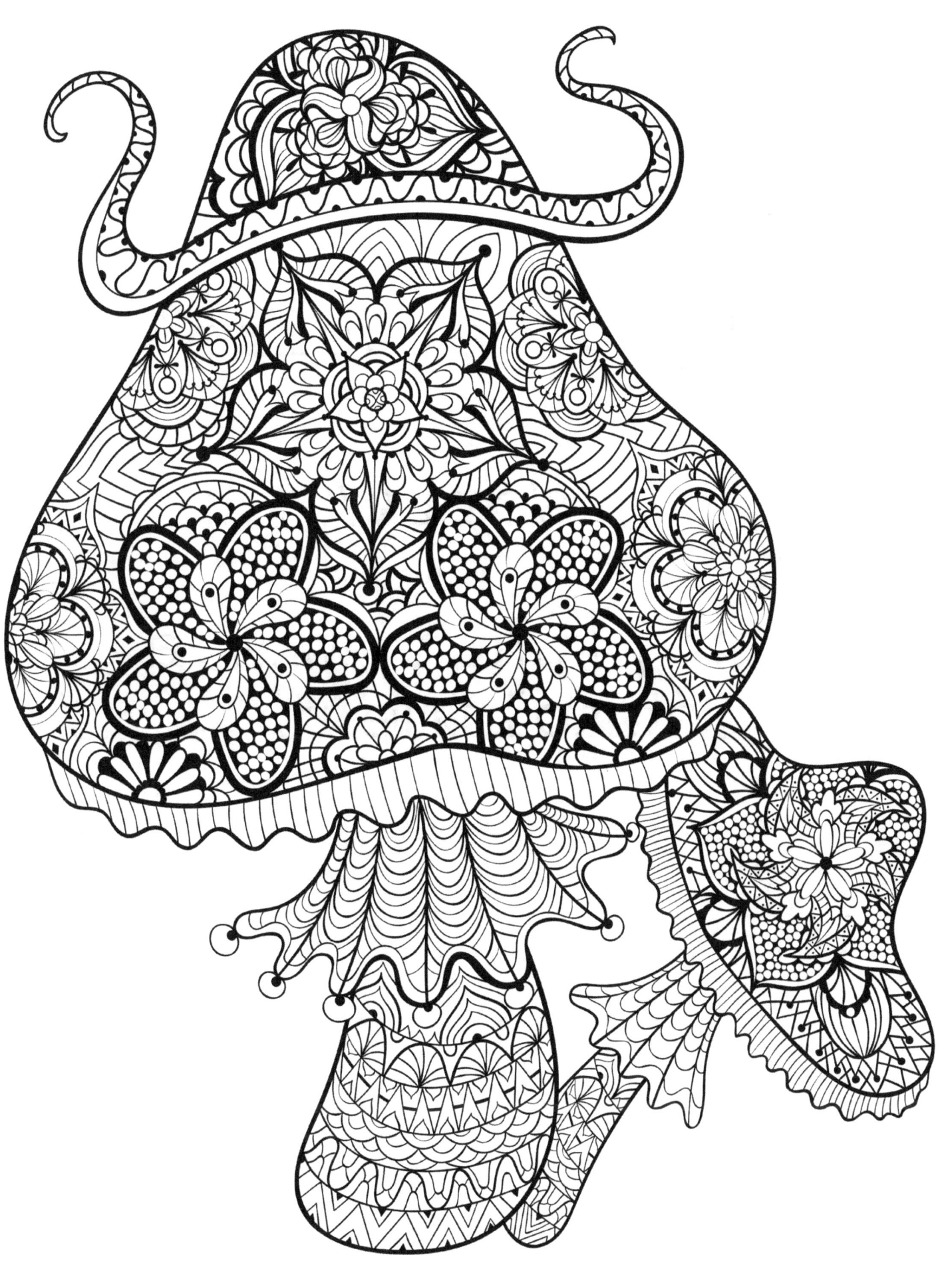

"you're weird"

"sorry"

"no, that was a
compliment"

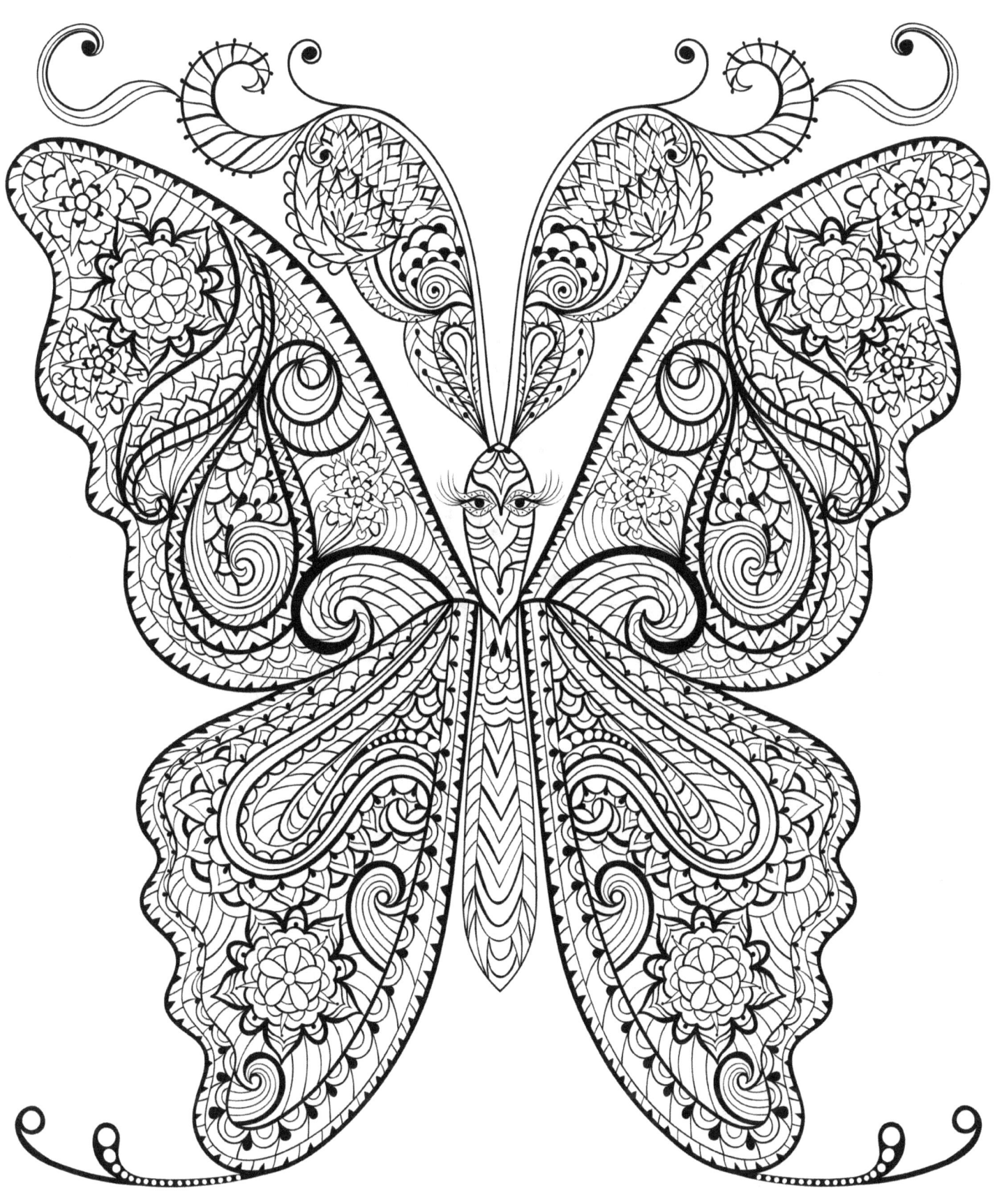

make your weird light
shine bright
so the other weirdos
know where to
find you

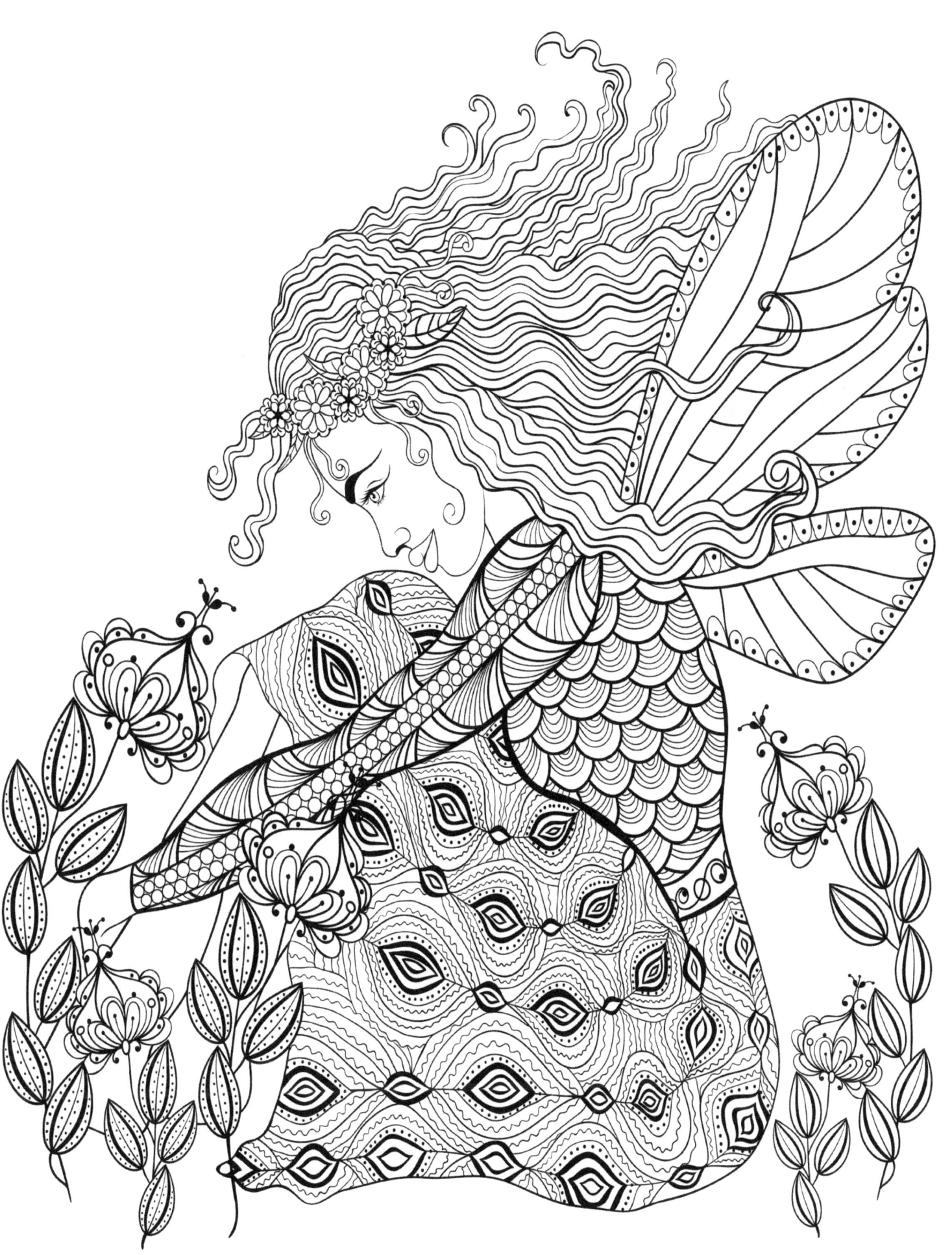

do whatever,
be weird, it's okay

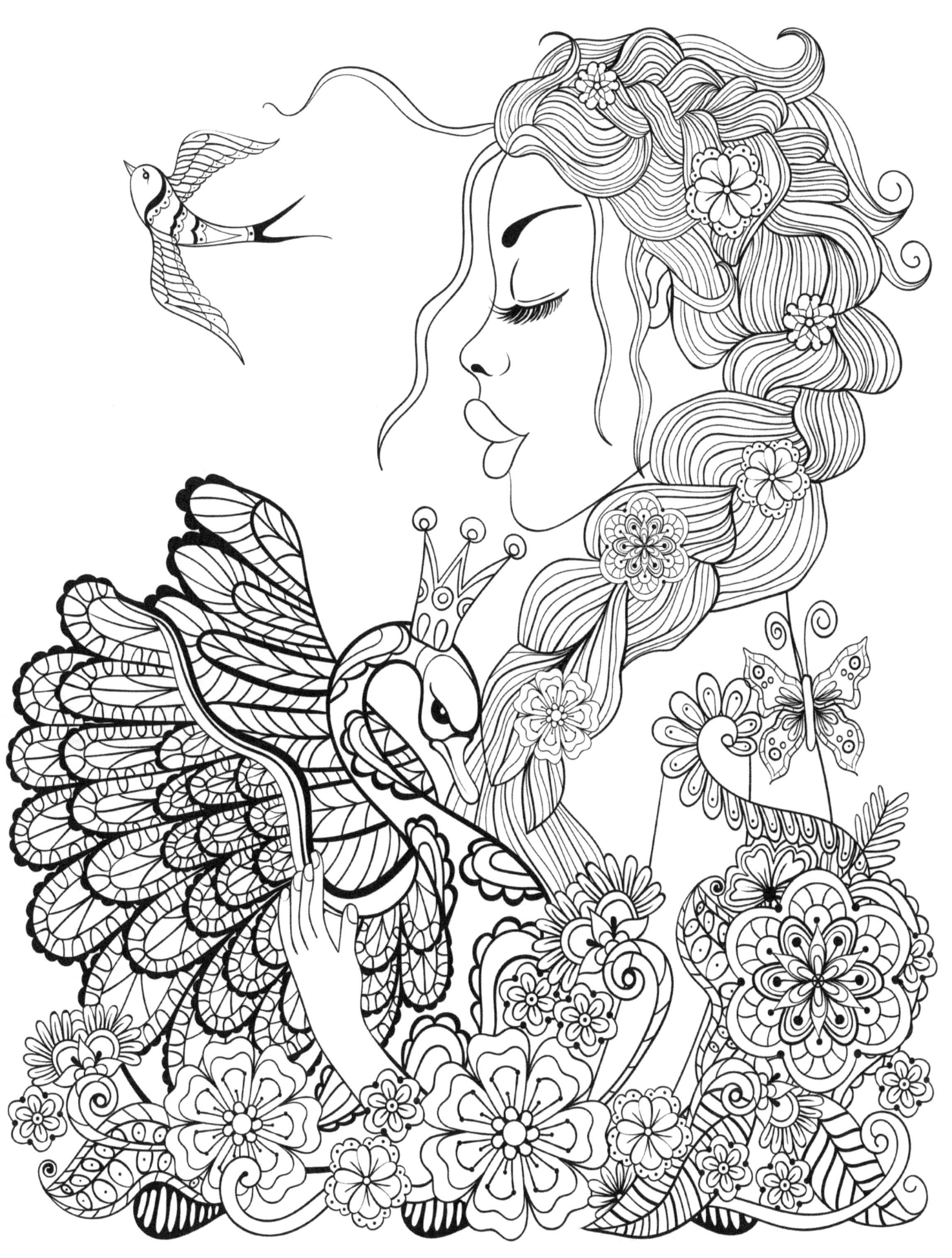

fall into
mutual weirdness
(it's called love)

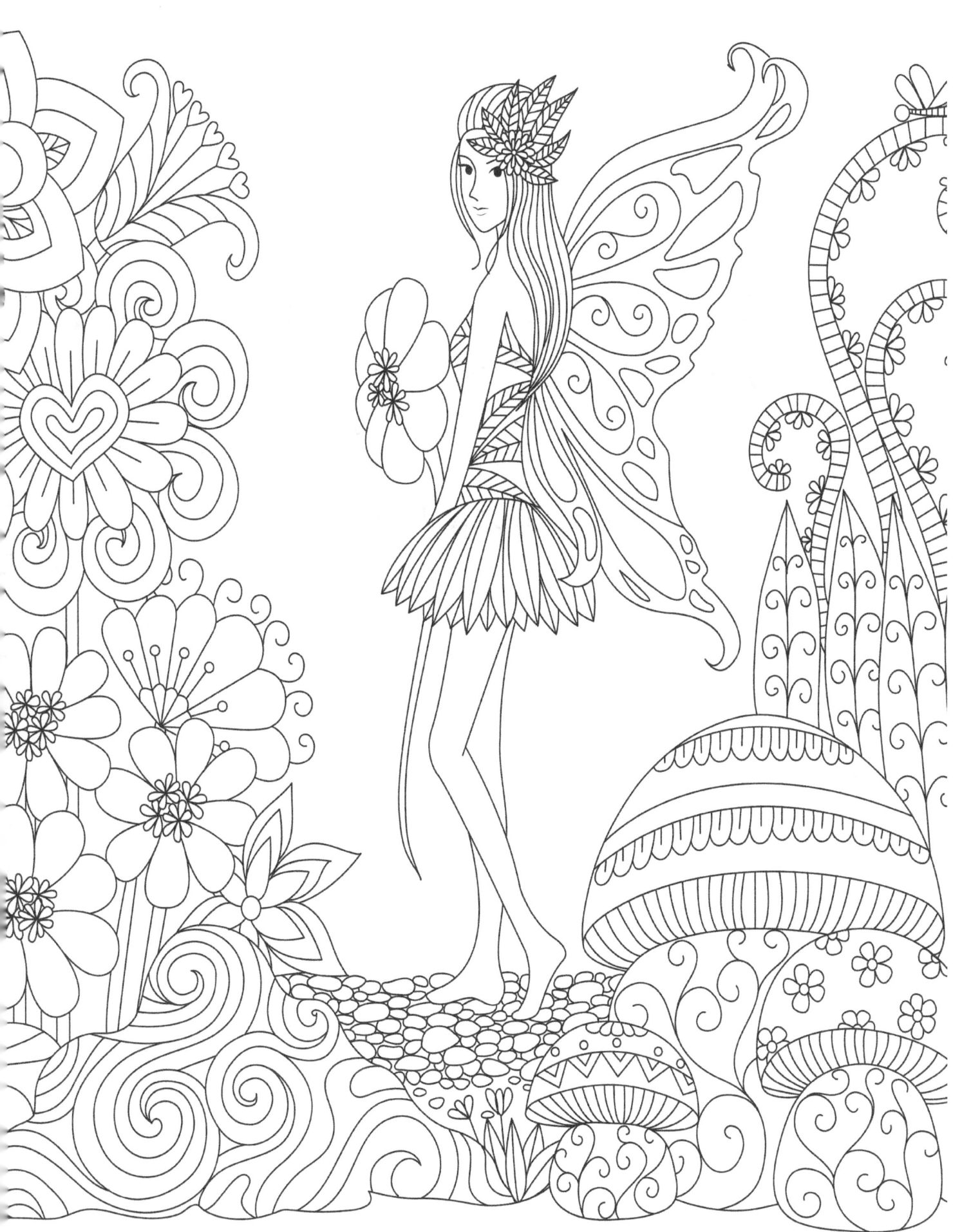

i like weird things,
weird is always
good, weird's always
different

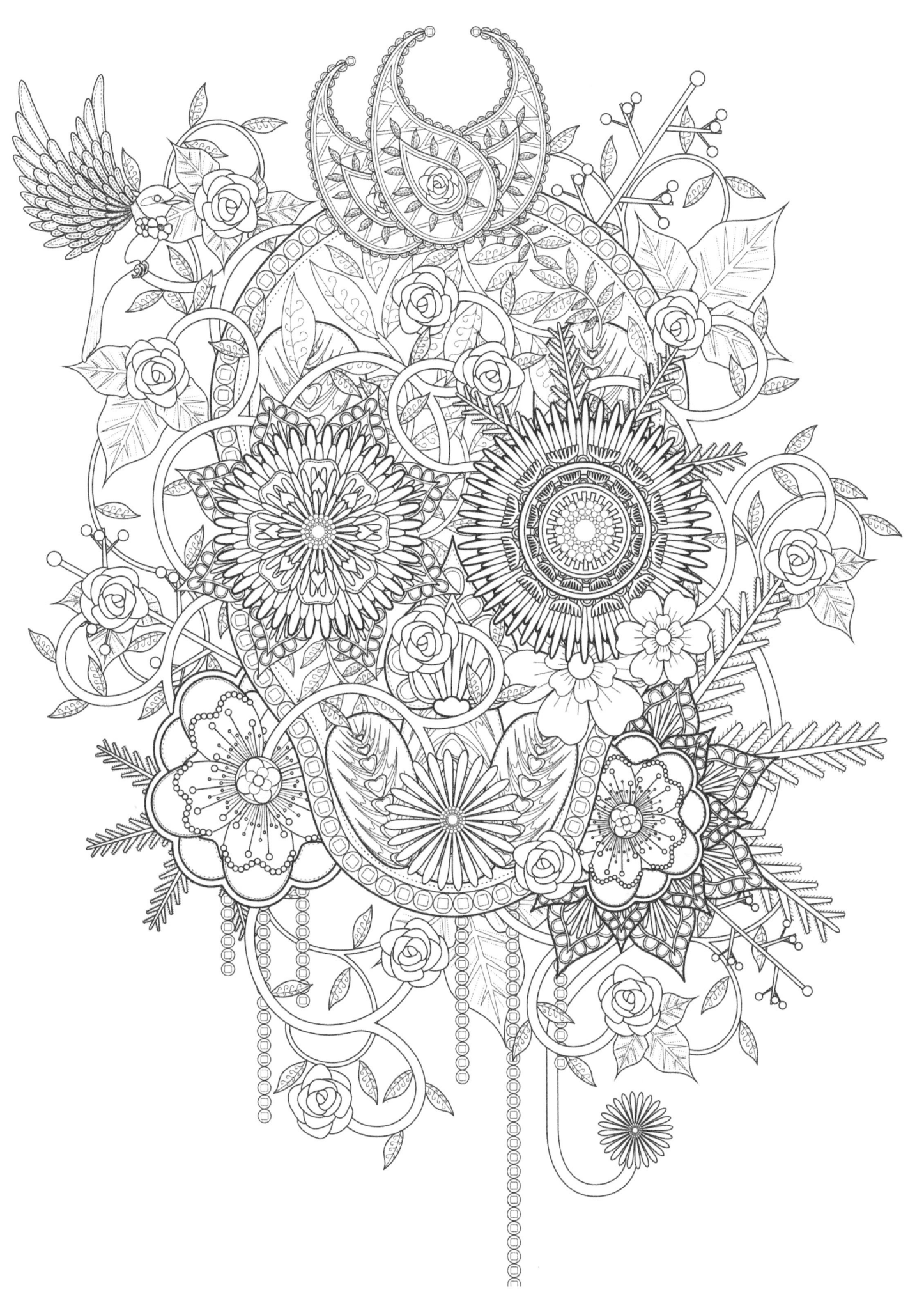

there's no beauty
without some
weirdness

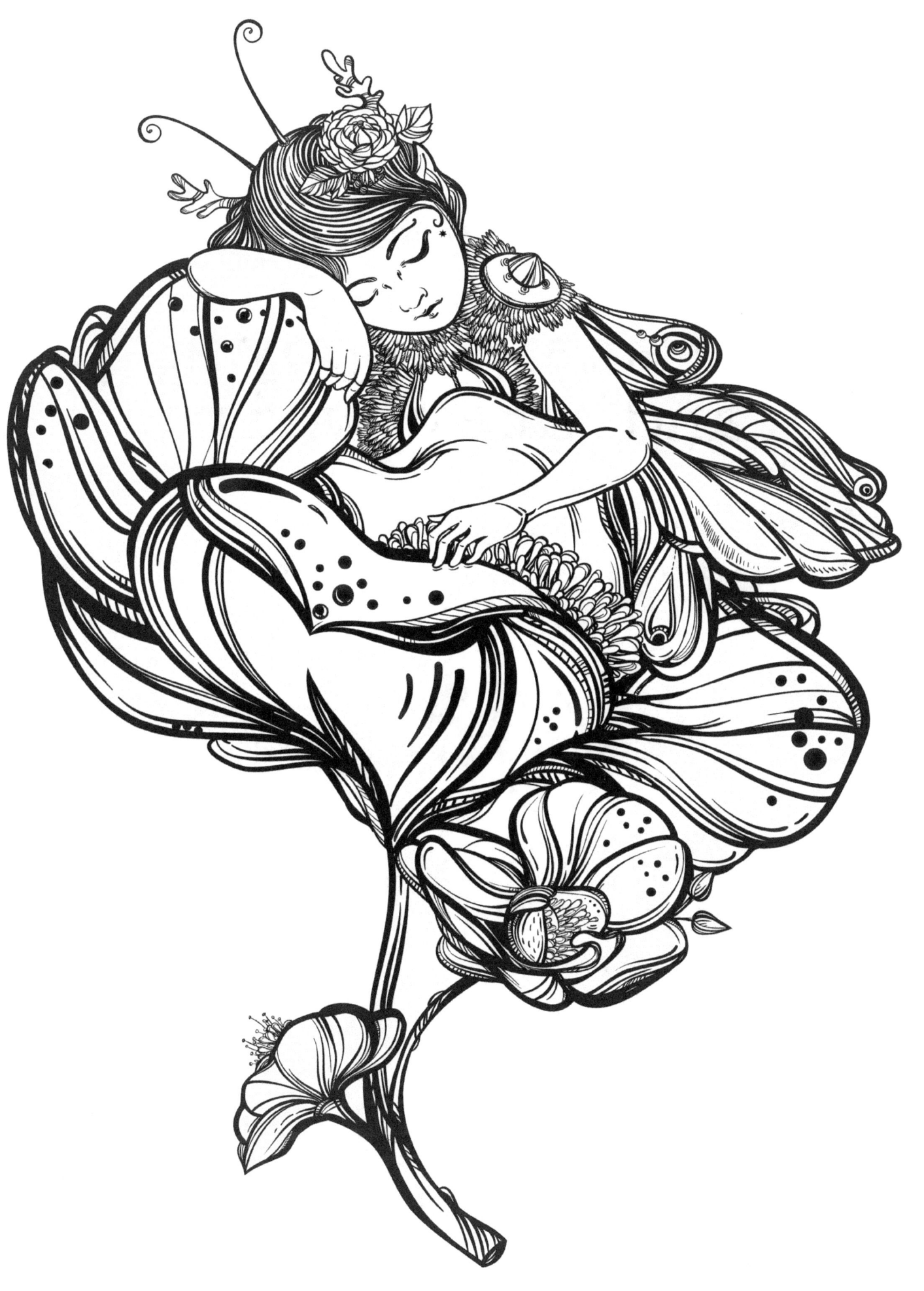

stay happy
and stay weird

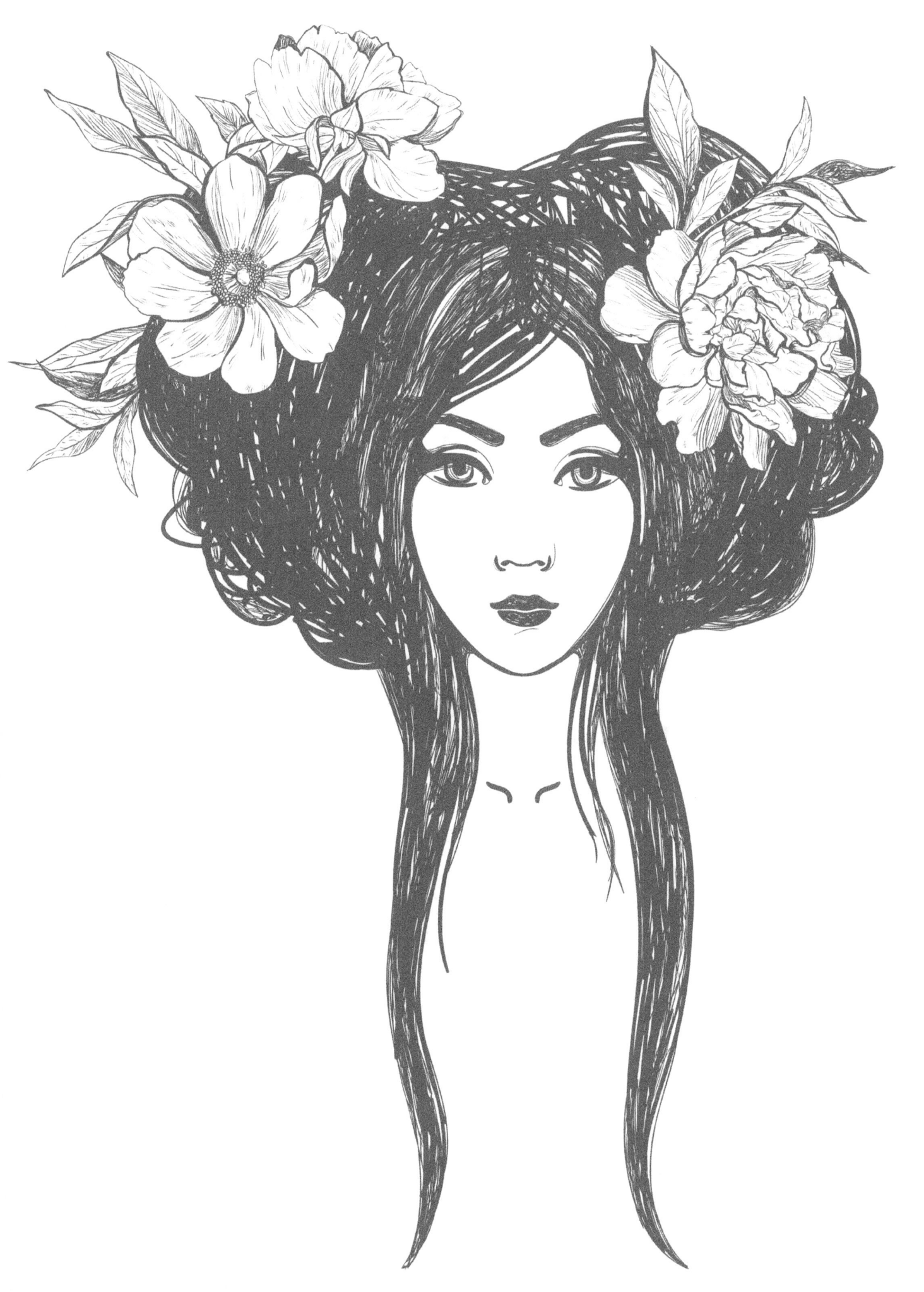

proud of being weird

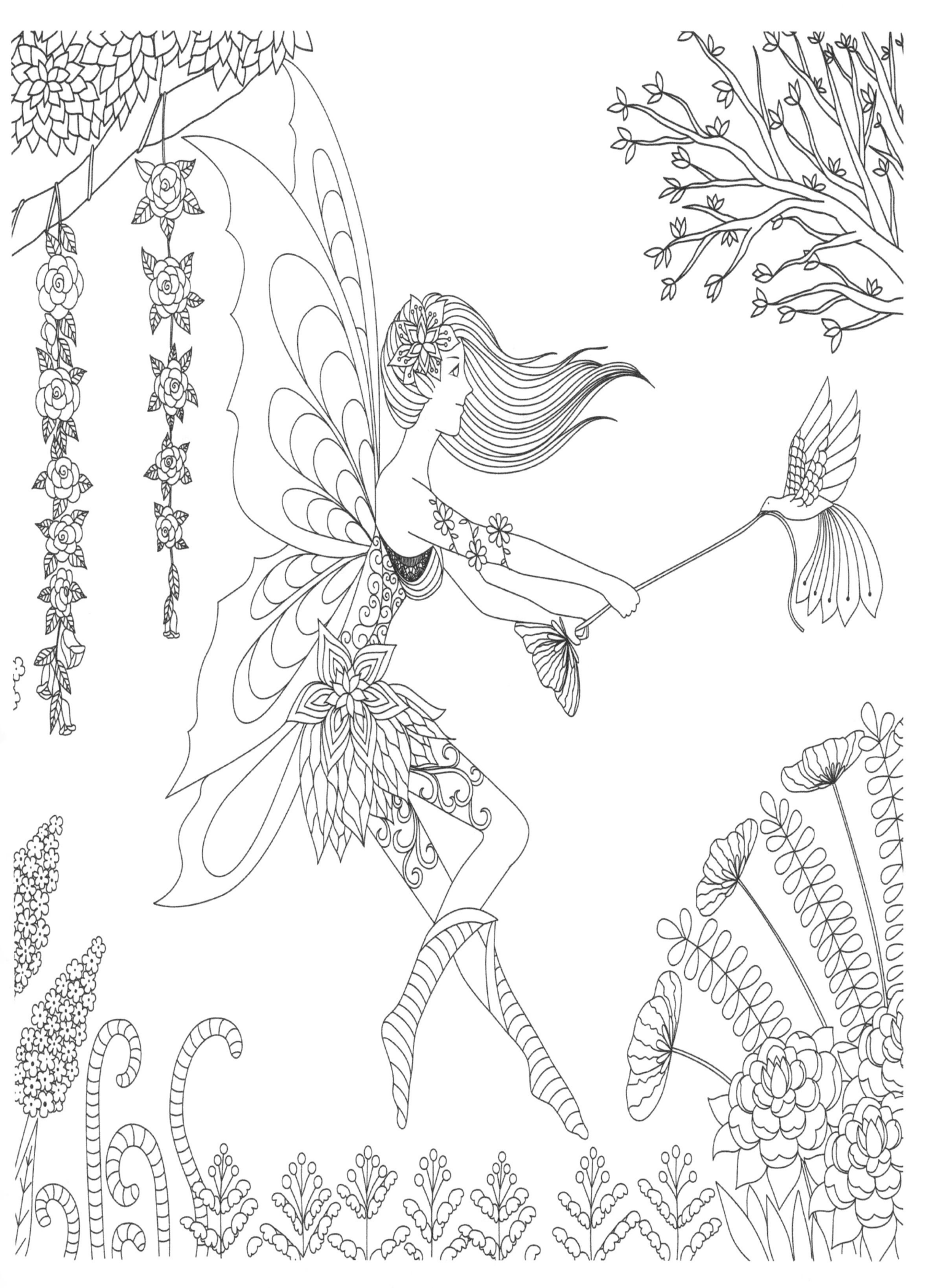

keep calm
and stay weird

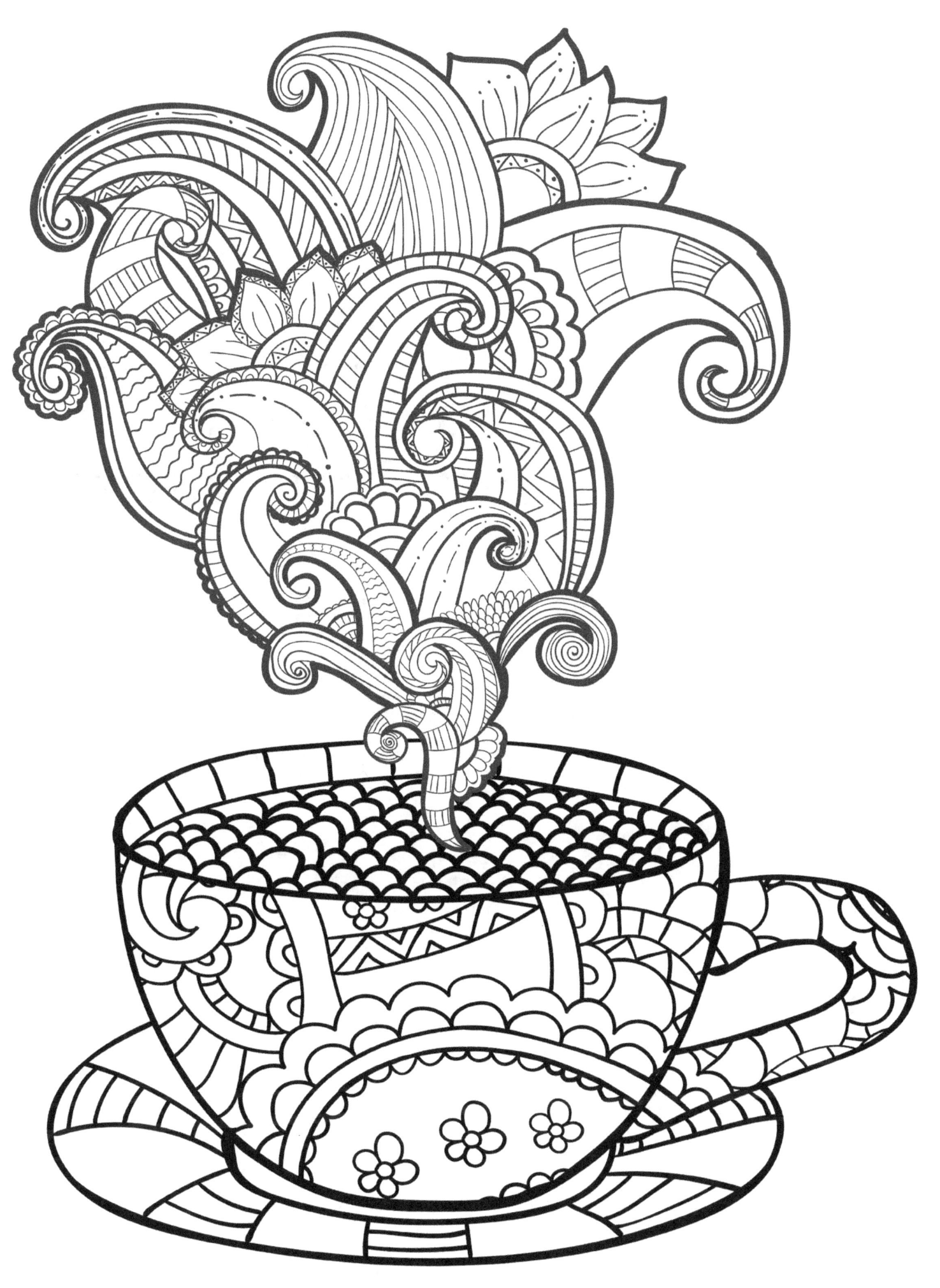

stay weird,
life is too short, to
be anything but happy

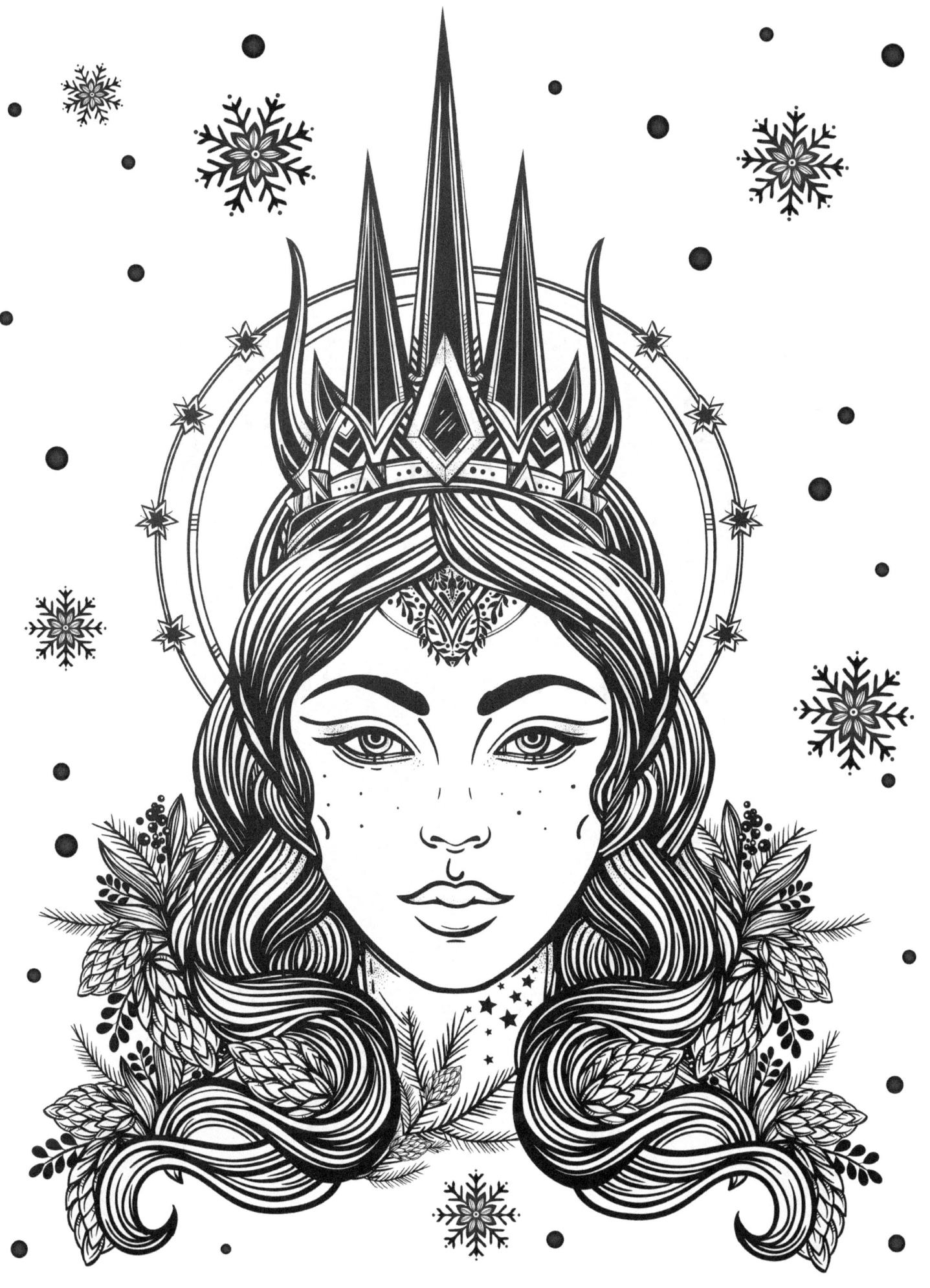

be weird,don't be
afraid of what anybody
thinks

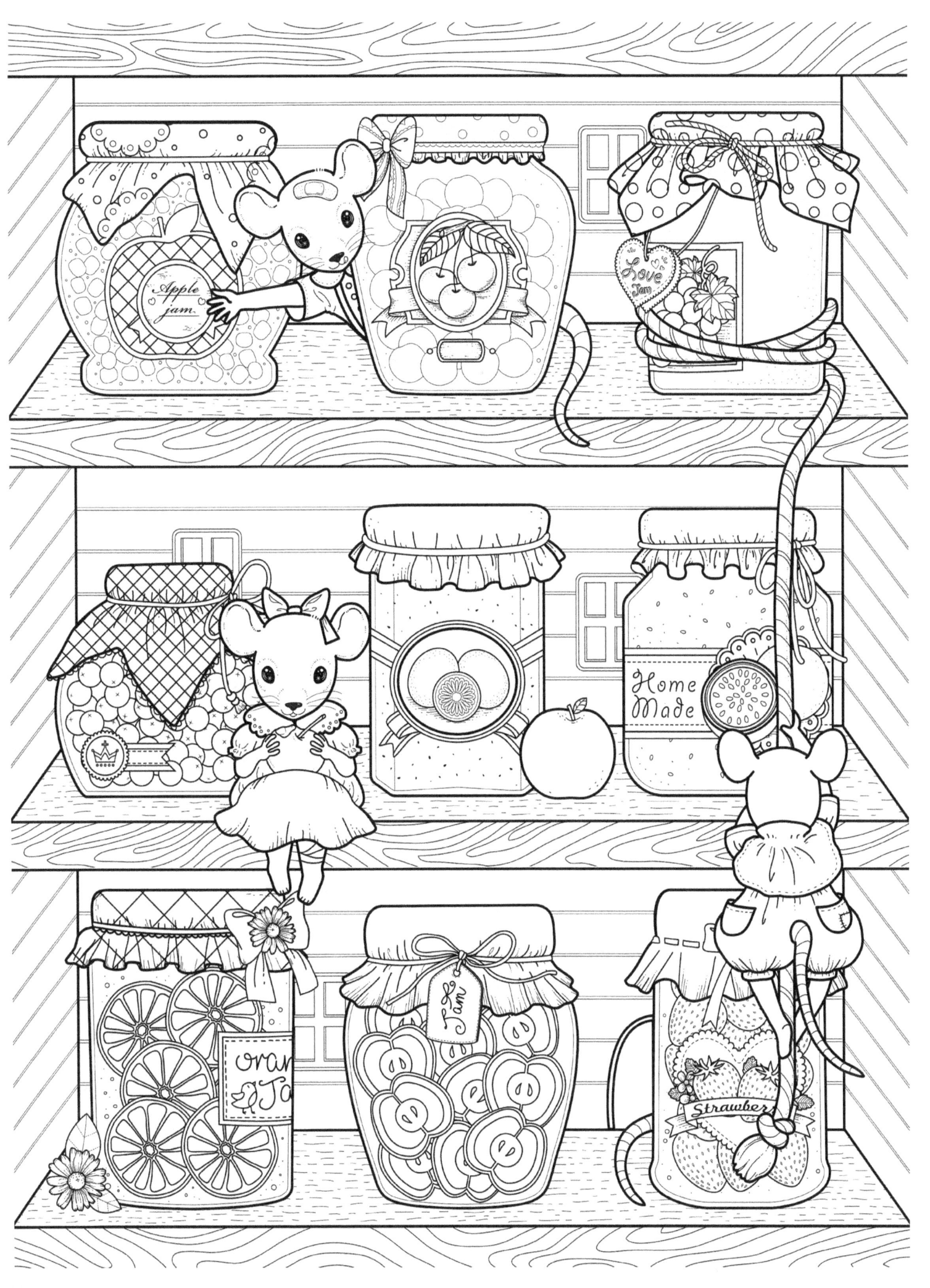

my favorite things
are weird things

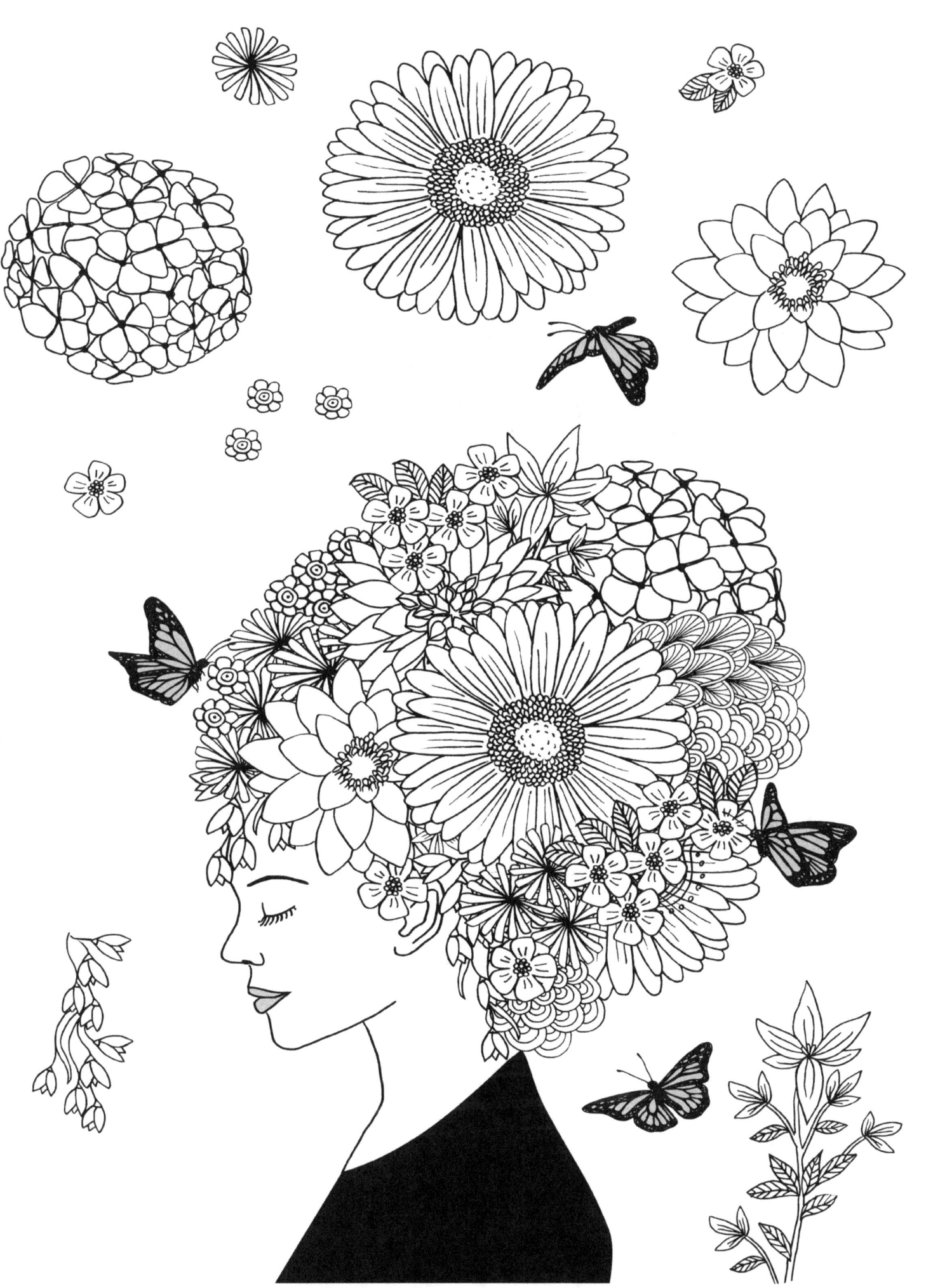

find yourself
and be that

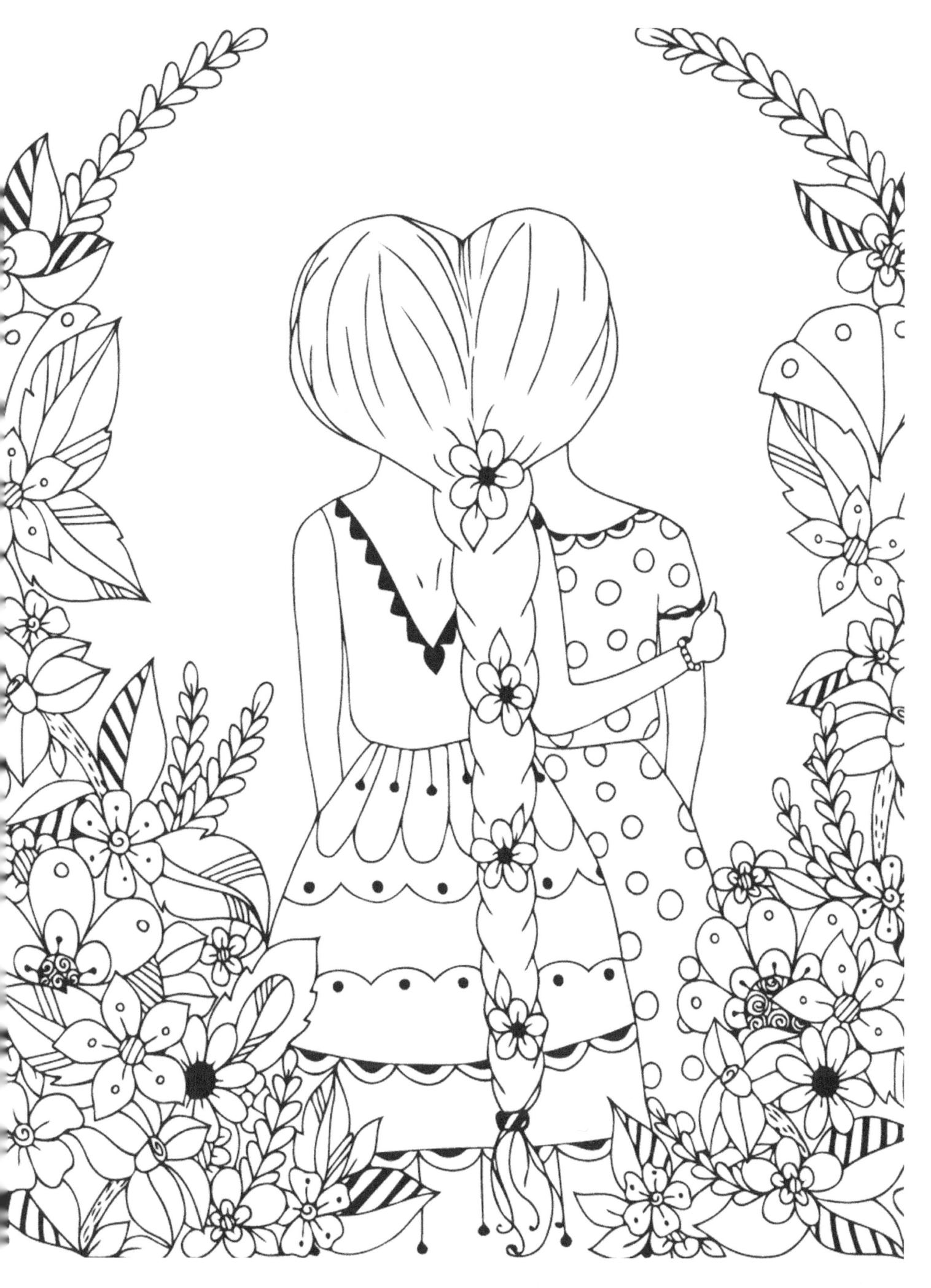

go where you feel
most alive

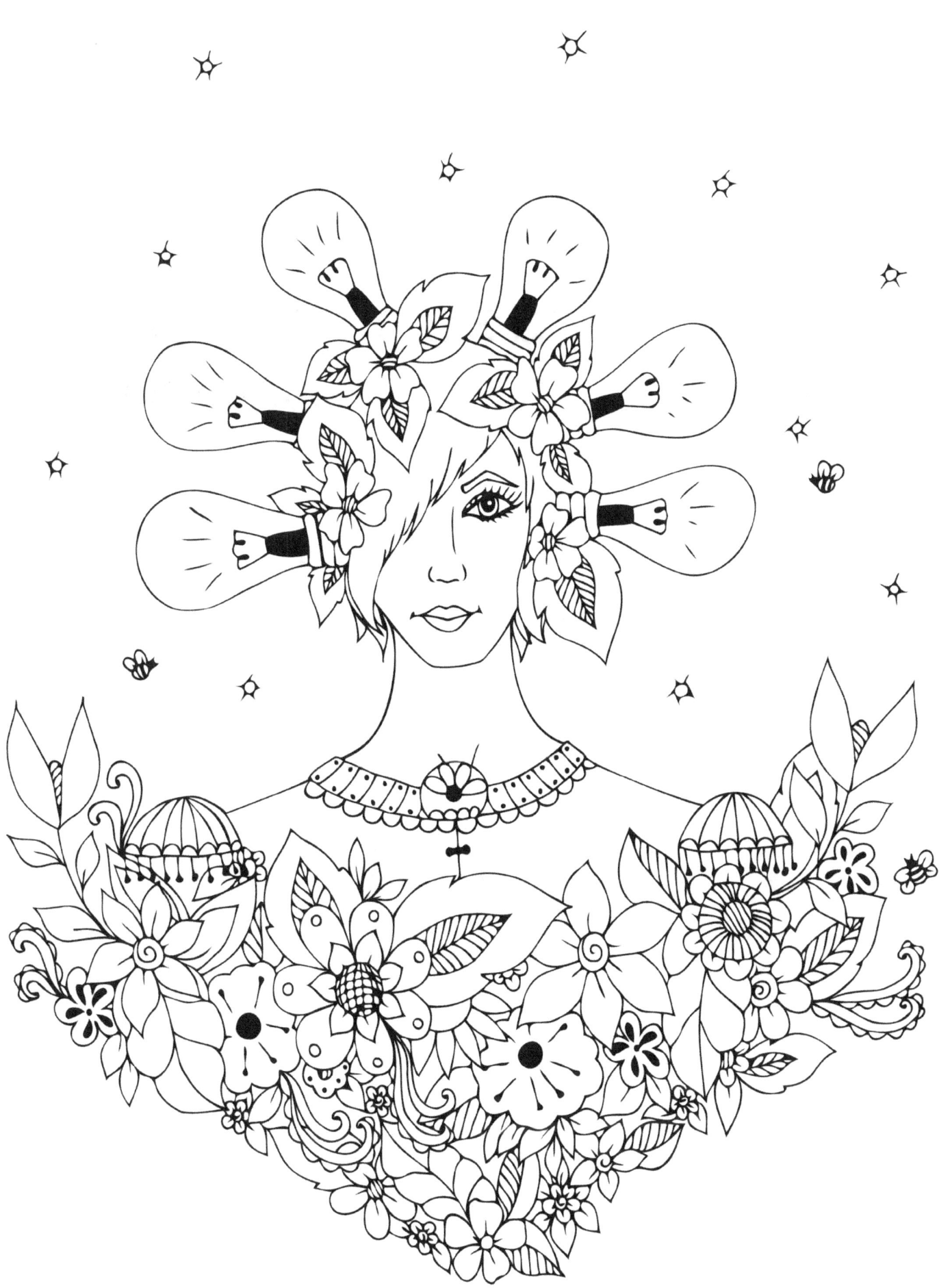

the weirdest people
are the best people

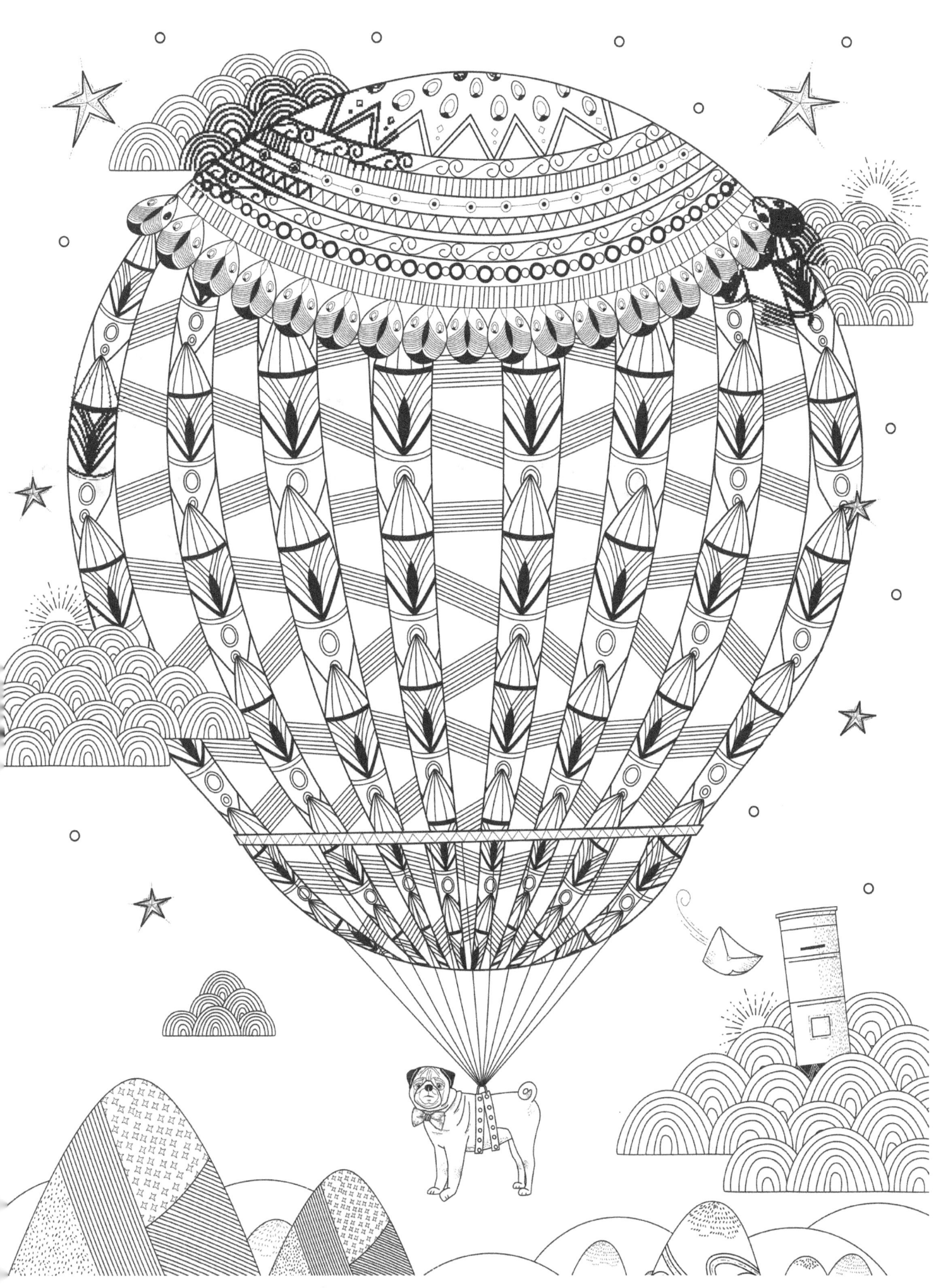

you may be accused
of many things in
life, don't let being
normal be one of them

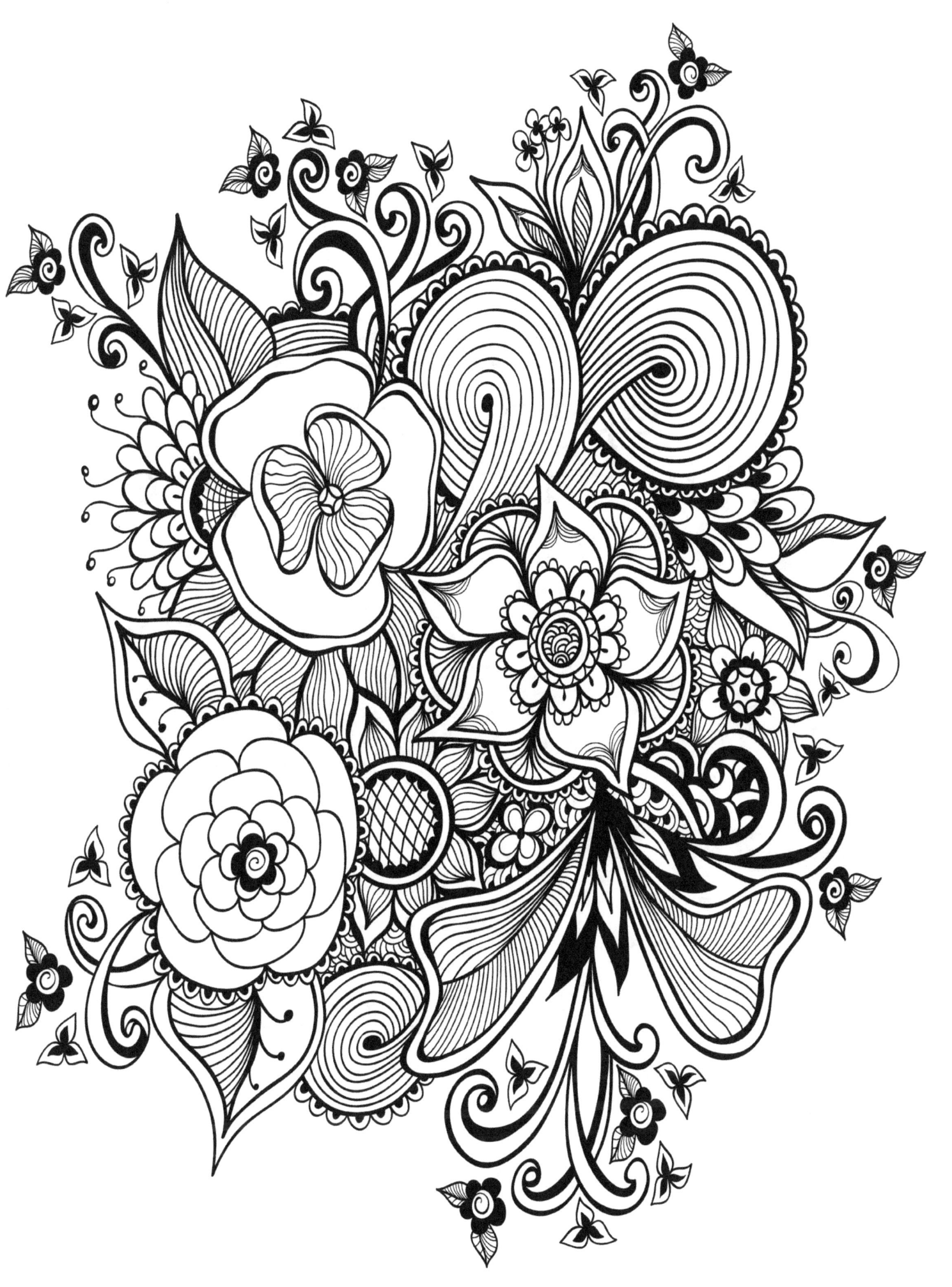

you can't do
epic sh*t
with basic people

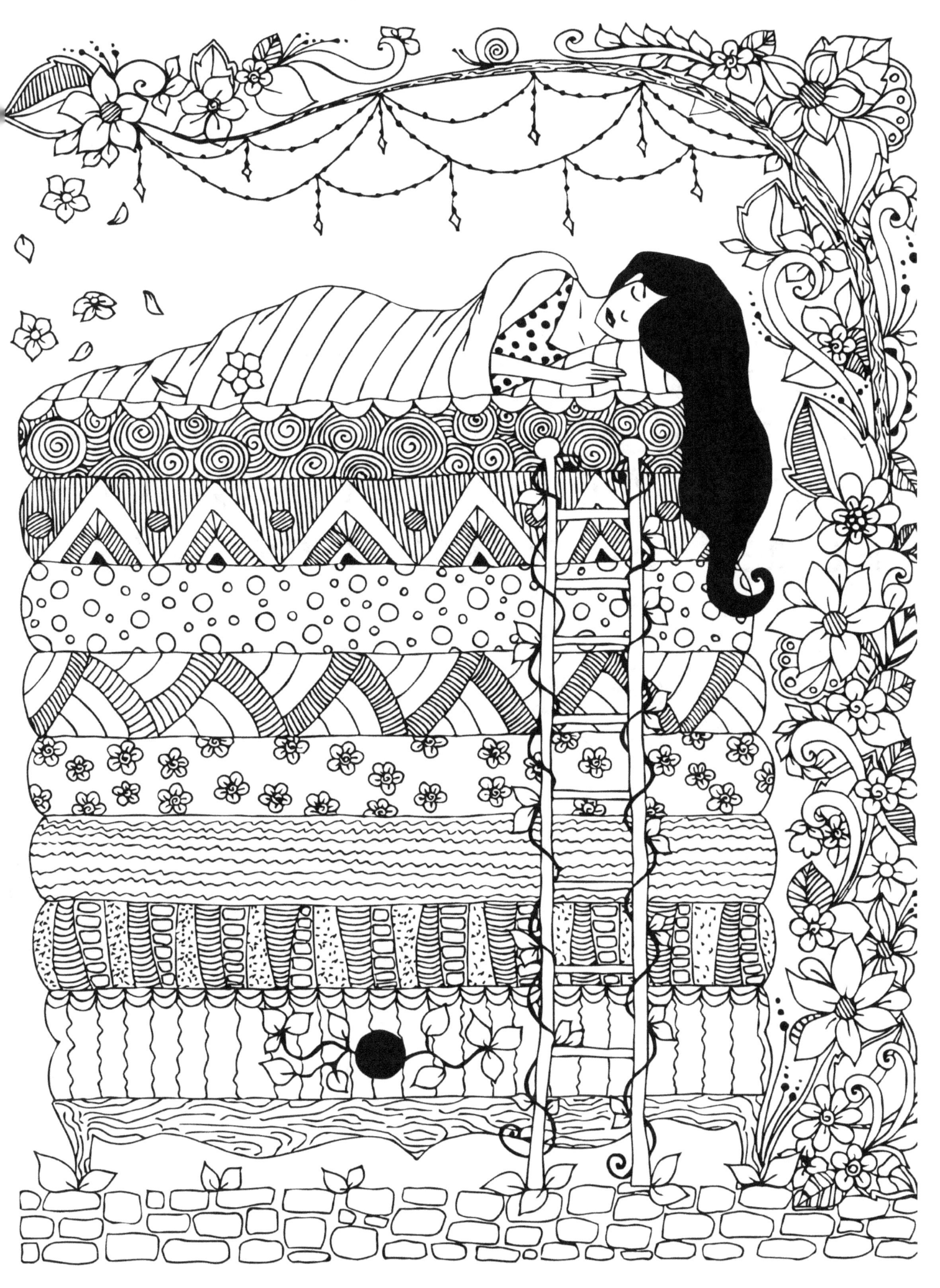

being called weird is
 the best because you
know you are not, the
same as everyone else

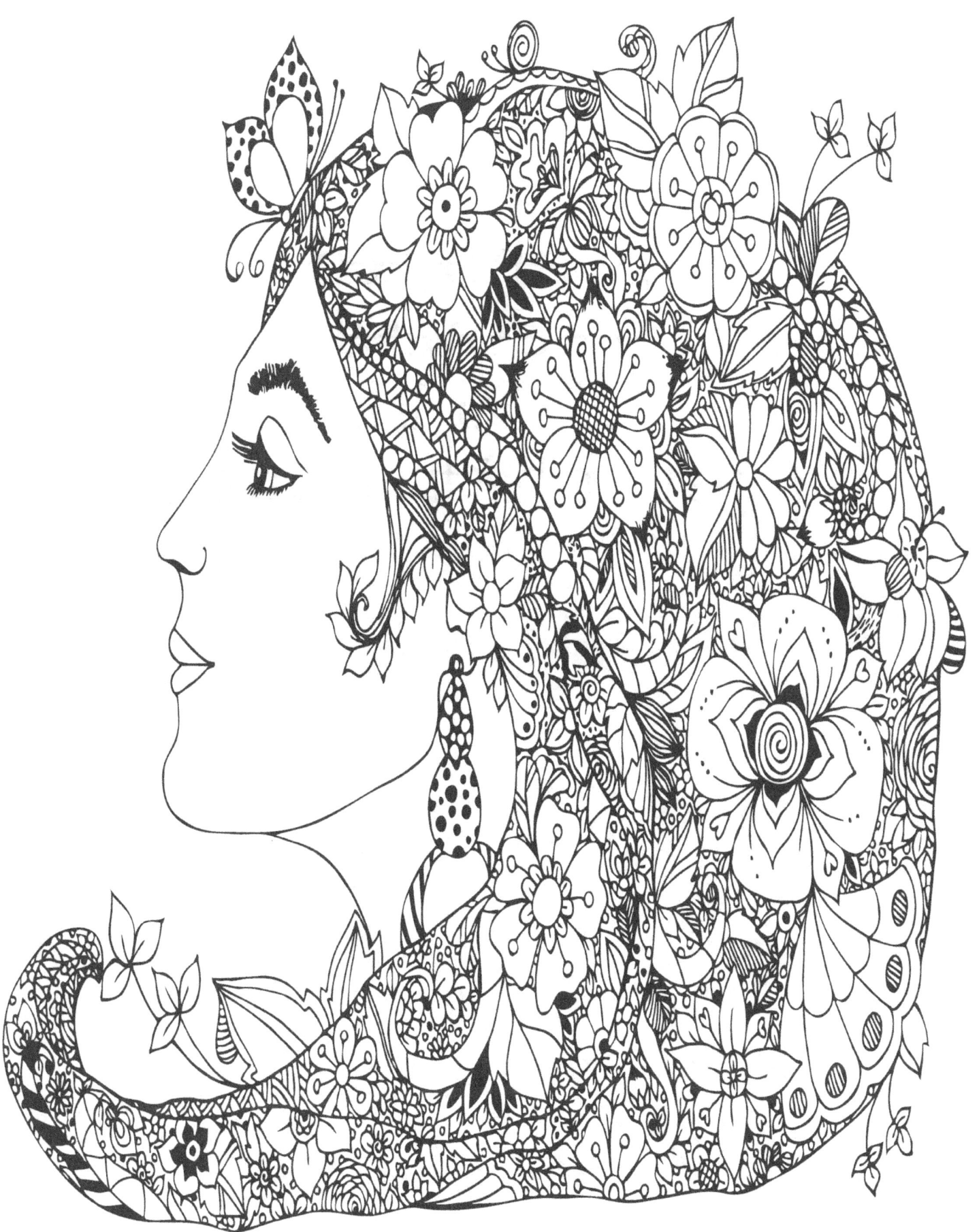

~~i should~~
~~i could~~
i will
(get sh*t done)

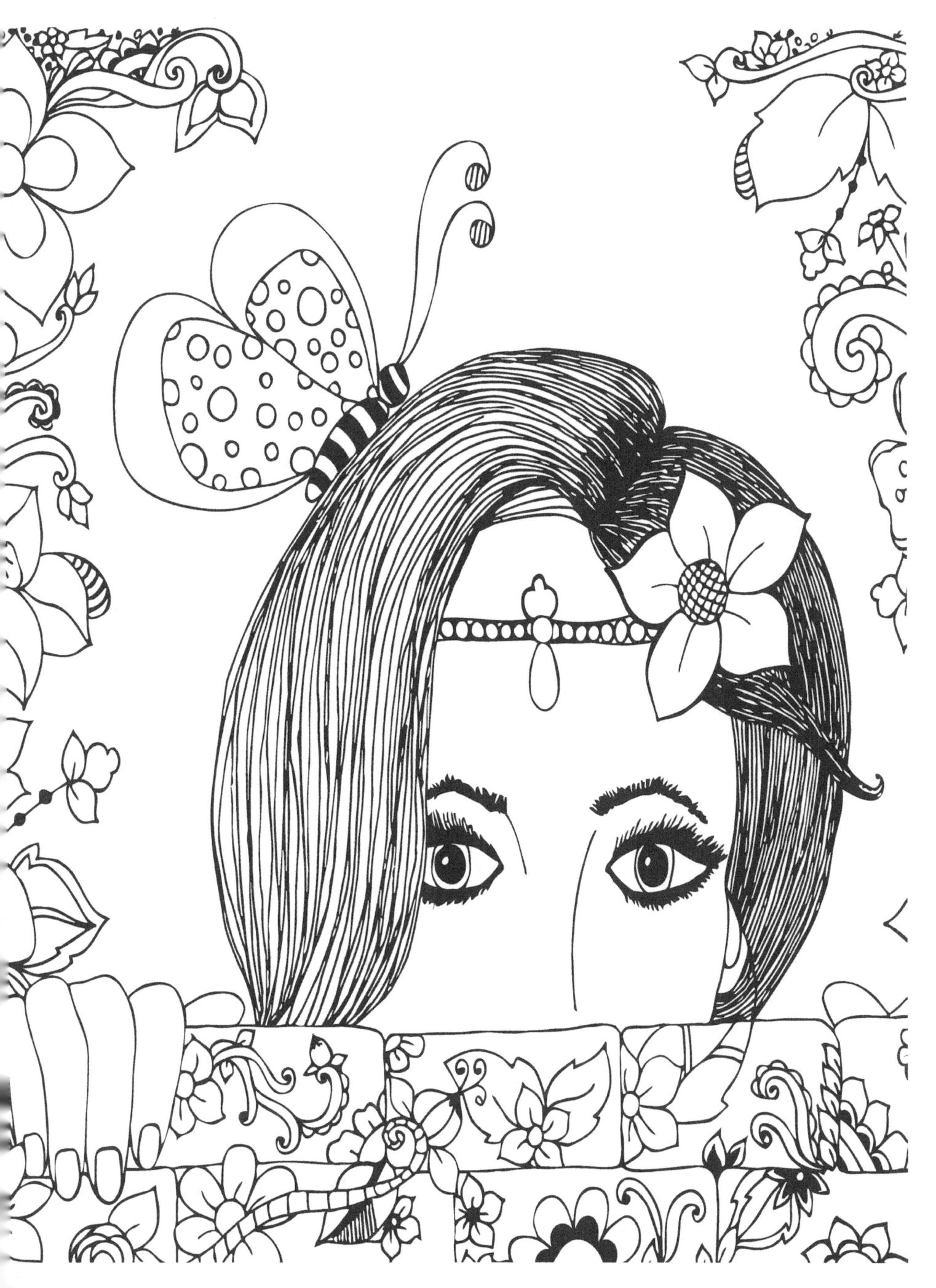

www.ingramcontent.com/pod-product-compliance
Lightning Source LLC
Chambersburg PA
CBHW080845170526
45158CB00009B/2635